© 1989 by Sunbelt Publications, Inc.
P.O. Box 191126
San Diego, CA 92159-1126
www.sunbeltbooks.com

Photography: Greg Lawson
Introduction: David Michaels
Captions: Greg Lawson
Art Director: Ralph Cernuda
Translations: Fabienne S. Chauderlot,
Margaret M. Posner, Roselinde Konrad
Typography: Creative Type Graphics

International Standard Book Number 0-916251-40-3
Library of Congress Catalog Card Number 89-085067
08 07 06 05   8 7 6 5

Printed in Singapore

Opuntia basilaris

PALM SPRINGS OASIS

You have to see it to believe it! Palm Springs and the Coachella Valley area continuously tantalizes residents and guests alike. Offering natural wonders and a myriad of beautiful hotels, restaurants and shops, this proud community has become world famous.

A dependable warm and sunny climate enhances the regional flavor, making it the ideal vacation spot. Outdoor enthusiasts enjoy a wide variety of activities including tennis, swimming, horseback riding and golf. Many notables can be seen regularly frequenting the lush green golf courses. For years Palm Springs has hosted filmmakers, entertainers, and various dignitaries.

The sightseeing opportunities are endless. Some of the most popular sights are the Joshua Tree National Monument, Salton Sea, Palm Springs Historical Museum, Moorton Botanical Gardens, and enchanting Indian Canyons. These wonders can be found just minutes from downtown Palm Springs. The most noted is Palm Canyon located in the Agua Caliente Reservations. Here you can hike meandering trails and experience a multitude of palms and silvery springs.

Perhaps the most breathtaking views are those from the Palm Springs Aerial Tramway extending from the Chino Canyon to the eastern portion of Long Valley. This extraordinary ride on one of the world's longest lifts climbs to an elevation of over 8000 feet. From the peak you can delight in a spectacular panorama of the mountains and the vast Coachella Valley.

In the spring desert flowers bloom in a brilliant array of colors. The violet desert verbena, hedgehog cactus, and the magnificent magenta beavertail are among the many varieties.

A different dimension of the valley's beauty lies in the rich agriculture. Each year the area yields impressive quantities of fruits and vegetables, including asparagus, grapes, and dates. Dates are grown on 5221 acres and harvest an incredible 2.5 tons per acre, making the valley one of the top producers of the fruit. The city of Indio takes credit for the majority of the date production.

In spite of their increasing popularity, the cities throughout the Coachella Valley have done a remarkable job of maintaining controlled growth. Where other towns fall short in the planning and zoning areas, the community leaders in these nine cities have developed building height restrictions, added new cross streets to alleviate congestion, and have preserved an overall charm by astute planning.

From the early days when many Cahuilla tribes first settled and built their homes from palm fronds, to its current more metropolitan posture, Palm Springs remains the desert jewel of the world . . . .**a beautiful oasis.**

PALM SPRINGS OASIS

¡Hay que ver para creer! Palm Springs y Coachella Valley siguen fascinando a sus residentes y a sus visitantes. Esta orgullosa comunidad se ha hecho mundialmente famosa por sus maravillas naturales y sus innumerables hoteles elegantes.

El continuo clima cálido y soleado realza su sabor regional convirtiéndolo en el centro vacacional ideal. Los amantes del aire libre pueden disfrutar de una gran variedad de actividades como el tenis, la natación, y el golf así como montar a caballo. Personalidades famosas regularmente frecuentan los hermosos prados de los campos de golf. Por muchos años, Palm Springs ha sido el anfitrión de cineastas y estrellas de Hollywood. Bob Hope, Frank Sinatra y el ex-presidente Gerald Ford son algunas de las celebridades que residen aquí.

Hay numerosas oportunidades de visitar puntos de interés. Algunos de los sitios más populares son Joshua Tree National Monument, Salton Sea, Palm Springs Historical Museum, Moorton Botanical Gardens y los atrayentes Indian Canyons. Estas maravillas están a unos minutos del centro de Palm Springs; la más famosa es Palm Canyon que se encuentra junto a Agua Caliente Reservation. Aquí uno puede andar por caminos sinuosos y admirar los manantiales plateados y una multitud de palmas.

Una de las vistas más impresionantes es la que se puede ver desde el Palm Springs Aerial Tramway que se extiende desde Chino Canyon hasta la parte este de Long Valley. Este paseo extraordinario en uno de los ascensores más largos del mundo sube a más de 8000 pies de altura. Desde la cima uno se deleita viendo el panorama espectacular de las montañas y el vasto Coachella Valley.

En la primavera, las flores desérticas se abren en un brillante despliegue de colores. La verbena violeta, el cacto erizo y el "beavertail" son algunas de las muchas especies que aquí crecen.

Otro factor que contribuye a la belleza del valle es su rica agricultura. Cada año esta área produce cantidades impresionantes de frutas y vegetales, como el espárrago, la uva y el dátil. Los dátiles crecen en 5221 acres y se cosechan 2.5 toneladas por cada acre. Este cifras han convertido al valle, especialmente a la ciudad de Indio, en uno de los productores más importantes del dátil.

A pesar de su creciente popularidad, las ciudades en todo Coachella Valley han logrado controlar su desarollo. En contraste con otras comunidades que se han quedado atrás en su planificación y zonificación urbana, los líderes municipales de estas nueve ciudades han legislado restricciones sobre la altura de edificios. También han abierto nuevas calles para descongestionar el tráfico y así preservar el encanto del lugar.

Desde la época en que muchas tribus cahuilla se establecieron y construyeron sus casas con palmas, hasta su actual carácter metropolita, Palm Springs continúa siendo la joya desértica del mundo....**un hermoso oasis.**

PALM SPRINGS OASIS

Il faut le voir pour le croire! Palm Springs, au coeur de la vallée Coachella, ne cesse de séduire ses habitants et ses hôtes. Grâce aux merveilles naturelles qu'elle offre, ainsi qu'à sa myriade de splendides hôtels, restaurants et boutiques, cette fière commune est devenue célèbre dans le monde entier.

Son climat éternellement doux et ensoleillé, qui met en valeur la qualité toute particulière de cette région, en fait un cadre de vacances idéal. Les amateurs de plein air peuvent se livrer à d'innombrables activités telles que, entre autres, le tennis, la natation, l'équitation ou le golf. De nombreuses stars fréquentent constamment les somptueux et verdoyants terrains de golf. Cela fait des années que Palm Springs acceuille réalisateurs de films et vedettes d'Hollywood. Parmi eux Bob Hope, Frank Sinatra et l'ancien Président Gerald Ford y ont élu résidence.

Les possibilités de promenade et de visites sont infinies. Parmi les plus populaires se trouvent le Monument National du 'Joshua Tree', la "mer" Salton, le Musée d'Histoire de Palm Springs, les Jardins Botaniques Moortor et les fascinants Canyons indiens. Toutes ces splendeurs sont à peine à quelques minutes du centre ville, y compris la plus renommée: le Palm Canyon à proximité de la Réserve Agua Caliente. C'est là que vous pourrez parcourir les sentiers sinueux de randonnée et découvrir les multiples sortes de palmiers et les nombreuses sources argentées.

La vision la plus incroyable est sans doute celle que l'on a depuis le tramway suspendu de Palm Springs qui s'étend entre le Canyon Chino et l'extrémité Est de Long Valley. Cette extraordinaire ballade dans l'un des plus longs téléphériques du monde vous emmènera à plus de 2400m d'altitude. Du sommet on peut apprécier un panorama spectaculaire des montagnes et de la large vallée Coachella.

Au printemps, le désert se couvre d'innombrables fleurs de toutes couleurs, comme celles des verveines violettes, du cactus 'hedgehog' et des magnifiques 'beavertail' magenta.

Un autre aspect de la beauté de la vallée réside en sa riche agriculture. Chaque année, la région produit fruits et légumes en quantités impressionnantes. Asperges, raisins et dates poussent à foison. Les dates sont cultivées sur 2100 hectares et on en récolte plus de 5 tonnes par hectare, ce qui fait de la vallée, et particuliérement de Chino qui en produit la plus grande partie, **l'un des** premiers producteurs de ce fruit.

Pourtant, malgré leur renommée qui ne cesse de grandir, les villes de la vallée ont réussi à contrôler de façon admirable leur expansion. Alors que d'autres villes sont incapables de restreindre leur urbanisation, les dirigeants de ces 9 cités ont au contraire établi de nombreux plans de protection: ils ont limité la hauteur des bâtiments, construit de nouvelles voies pour alléger le trafic urbain et préservent ainsi astucieusement tout le charme de leurs communautés.

Depuis son origine, quand de nombreuses tribus indiennes Cahuilla s'y sont établlies et y ont construit leur demeures en feuilles de palmiers, jusqu'à aujourd'hui oú elle tient sa place de veritable métropole, Palm Springs a toujours été - et elle le reste - **le joyau du désert américain.**

PALM SPRINGS OASIS

Es ist fast nicht zu beschreiben - man muß es gesehen haben! Palm Springs und das Tal Coachella üben auf Besucher wie Bewohner nach wie vor einen ungeheuren Reiz aus. Mit ihren Naturschönheiten und den ungezählten attraktiven Hotels, Restaurants und Läden ist diese einzigartige Stadt in aller Welt berühmt geworden.

Hinzu kommt das charakteristische gleichbleibend warme und sonnige Klima, das Palm Springs und Umgebung zum idealen Aufenthaltsort für Urlauber macht. Es bietet dem Sportbegeisterten eine Menge von Möglichkeiten, vom Schwimmen und Reiten zum Tennis-und vor allem Golfspielen. Auf den gepflegten Grunflächen der Golfplätze spielen regelmäßig vielerlei namhafte Leute. Überhaupt finden sich in Palm Springs seit Jahren Filmproduzenten und Hollywoodgrößen ein. Zu den Berühmtheiten, die dort auch wohnen, zählen Bob Hope, Frank Sinatra und der ehemalige Präsident Gerald Ford.

Die Ausflugsgelegenheiten in die Umgebung sind nahezu unbegrenzt. Besonders beliebt zu Besichtigungen sind das Joshua Tree National Monument, die Salton Sea, das Historische Museum von Palm Springs, der Moorton Botanische Garten und die faszinierenden Indian Canyons. Und alle diese Sehenswürdigkeiten sind nur Minuten vom Stadtzentrum entfernt. Die berühmteste ist der nahe der Aqua Caliente Reservation gelegene Palm Canyon, den man über gewundene Pfade durchwandern kann, oft unter Palmen und begleitet von silbrigen Quellen.

Den vielleicht atemberaubendsten Blick hat man von der Schwebebahn (der Palm Springs Aerial Tramway), die das Chino Canyon mit dem östlichen Teil des Tales (des Long Valley) verbindet. Diese unvergleichliche Fahrt auf einer der längsten Seilbahnen der Welt führt bis auf eine Höhe von über 2400 m. Vom Gipfel aus genießt man dann den Blick auf das großartige Panorama der Berge und das weite Coachella-Tal.

Im Frühjahr sprießen überall die wildwachsenden Blumen und bedecken weite Flächen mit ihren leuchtenden Blüten, darunter vielerlei bunten, vor allem violetten Wüstenpflanzen und Kakteen.

Ein anderer Aspekt der Schönheit dieses Tales rührt her von seiner umfassenden landwirtschaftlichen Nutzung. Die jährliche Obst- und Gemüseernte dieser Gegend ist beachtlich, vor allem an Spargel, Trauben und Datteln. Letztere werden auf einer Fläche von etwa 2090 Hektar Land angebaut und ergeben die unerhörte Menge von 6 Tonnen Früchten pro Hektar. Die Stadt Indio kann sich dabei als erstrangig im Dattelanbau rühmen.

Trotz ihrer wachsenden Popularität ist es den Städten im Coachella-Tal gelungen, unerwünschtes unkontrolliertes Anwachsen zu verhindern. Während andere Orte bei ihrer Städteplanung und Zonenabgrenzung vielfach versagten, begrenzten diese neun Städte zum Beispiel die Höhe der Neubauten, planten zusätzliche Straßen zur Behebung von Verkehrsstauungen und bemühten sich durch kluge Voraussicht ganz allgemein darum, den besonderen Charme der Stadt zu erhalten.

Nicht zuletzt deshalb bleibt Palm Springs von seinen ersten Anfängen an, als sich viele Stämme der Cahuila-Indianer dort niederließen und Hütten aus Palmwedeln bauten, bis zu seinem heutigen städtischen Charakter der Inbegriff eines „Juwels in der Wüste", **eine wunderschöne Oase.**

PALM SPRINGS

OASIS

A GREG LAWSON PHOTOGRAPHIC PORTFOLIO
OF THE COACHELLA VALLEY REGION

9

Hundreds of thousands of date palms have helped make the
Coachella Valley the date capital of North America.

Cientos de miles de palmas han convertido a Coachella
Valley en el principal productor del dátil en Norteamérica.

Les palmiers-datiers par centaines de milliers ont fait de la vallée
Coachella la capitale de la date en Amérique du Nord.

Hunderttausende von Dattelpalmen haben dazu beigetragen, das
Tal von Coachella zum Hauptgebiet der nordamerikanischen
Dattelindustrie zu machen.

Brittlebush and verbena share the glory of a spring show of color.

"Brittlebush" y Verbena comparten la belleza de una
manifestación primaveral de colores.

Brittlebush et Verveine offrent ensemble un magnifique
spectacle de couleurs au printemps.

„Brittlebush" und Verbena wetteifern miteinander, wenn sie im
Frühjahr ihre Farben zur Schau stellen.

11

Dry weeds on sandy scarp near Indio Mountain.

Maleza seca en un declive arenoso cerca de Indio Mountain.

Herbes sèches sur un escarpement sableux, près de la montagne Indio.

Trockenes Kraut auf einer sandigen Böschung in Nähe des Indio-Gebirges.

A summer view of the majestic San Jacintos.

Una vista veraniega de las majestuosas montañas San Jacinto.

Eté. Vue des majestueuses montagnes San Jacintos.

Sommerlicher Blick auf das majestätische San-Jacintos-Gebirge.

Sunburst through Smoke Tree veil near Haystack Mountain.

Un rayo de sol atraviesa un velo de Smoke Trees cerca de
Haystack Mountain.

Le soleil transperce le voile d'un Smoke Tree.
Région des montagnes Haystack.

Sonnenstrahlen brechen durch einen Baum und verhüllen den
Haystack-Berg im Hintergrund.

Summer blossoms in desert wash, Painted Canyon.

Flores veraniegas en un aluvión desértico, Painted Canyon.

Floraisons d'été dans les fonds du désert, Painted Canyon.

Sommerliche Blüten in einem Wüstenschwemmgrund im Painted Canyon.

16

Rains stimulate the formation of long clusters of bright red flowers on the distinctive Ocotillo.

Las lluvias estimulan la formación de ramilletes alargados con brillantes flores rojas en el ocotillo.

Les averses permettent la formation de longues grappes de fleurs d'un rouge écarlate, tout en haut des Ocotillos si typiques.

Der Regen bringt die langen Dolden hellroter Blüten an den charakteristischen Ocotillo-Büschen sum Sprießen.

Teddy Bear Cholla and withered brittlebush bear mid-summer
heat on the east slope of the San Jacinto Range.

Teddy Bear Cholla y "brittlebush" marchito reciben el calor
veraniego en la cuesta este de San Jacinto Range.

Le Cholla aux formes d'ours en peluche et les Brittlebush
desséchés supportent la chaleur du plein été sur les
pentes Est de la chaine du San Jacinto.

Die sogenannten Teddybärkakteen und welken Brittle-büsche
ertragen die Hochsommerhitze auf den östlichen Hängen
der San-Jacintos-Gebirgskette.

18

Dawn reveals fresh winter powder on San Jacinto Mountains.

El amanecer descubre la nieve recién caída sobre las montañas San Jacinto.

La lumière de l'aube révèle les poudres fraiches des
premières neiges d'hiver sur les monts San Jacintos.

Die Morgendämmerung enthüllt den letzten Schnee auf den
Bergspitzen des Jacintos-Gebirges.

Desert Chicory

High desert starburst in Jumbo Rocks, Joshua Tree National Monument.

Manto de estrellas en el desierto alto visto desde Jumbo Rocks,
Joshua Tree National Monument.

Eclats de lumière dans le haut désert à Jumbo Rocks.
Joshua Tree National Monument.

Strahlendurchbruch über der Bergwüste in Jumbo Rock,
Joshua Tree National Monument.

Trichocereus sp.

A new desert showcase, Palm Springs Convention Center.

Un nuevo atractivo desértico, Palm Springs Convention Center.

Une nouvelle pièce dans le désert: le Centre de Conventions de Palm Springs.

Ein neues Prunkstück in Palm Springs, das Convention Center.

Fountain at dusk, Palm Springs Regional Airport.

Fuente al obscurecer, Palm Springs Regional Airport.

Fontaine au crépuscule, Aéroport régional de Palm Springs.

Brunnen bei Abenddämmerung am Regional-Flughafen von Palm Springs.

22

Adolescent Joshua Tree flowering in the Mojave,
Joshua Tree National Monument.

Un Joshua Tree adolescente floreciendo en el desierto Mojave,
Joshua Tree National Monument.

Jeune Joshua Tree en fleurs dans le Mojave,
Joshua Tree National Monument.

Junge blühende Yucca in der Jojave-Wüste,
Joshua-Tree-National-Monument-Park.

Brilliant color splash results from a profusion of Beavertail blossoms.

Las abandantes flores del cacto "beavertail" producen un
estallido de color.

Les nombreux 'cactus-beavertail' éclaboussent le désert de
leurs touches de couleurs brillantes.

Die leuchtend bunten Farbflecke rühren von den unzähligen
Blüten der Wüstenkakteen her.

24

Wind erosion created irregular patterns in this sand hill near Indian Wells.

La erosión del viento creé formas irregulares en una loma arenosa cerca de Indian Wells.

L'érosion due au vent a creé des dessins irréguliers sur
cette dune de sable près de Indian Wells

Durch Winderosion hervorgerufene unregelmäßige Muster in
einem sandigen Hang bei Indian Wells.

25

Bighorn sheep strains to feed on Palo Verde branches.

Un carnero se esfuerza para comer de las ramas de un Palo Verde.

Les moutons Bighorn recherchent de la nourriture sur les branches de Palo Verde.

Ein großhörniges Schaf bemüht sich um Futter von den Palo-Verde-Zweigen.

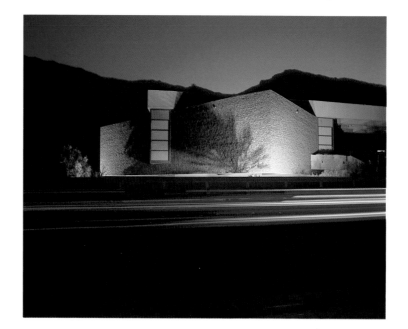

26

Palm Springs Desert Museum is the region's major
cultural arts center.

Palm Springs Desert Museum es el centro cultural más
importante de la región.

Le Musée du Désert de Palm Springs est le Centre Culturel
et Artistique principal de la région.

Das Palm-Springs-Desert-Museum ist das Hauptzentrum für
Kultur und Kunst dieser Gegend.

27

A nocturnal view of Palm Desert from Seven Level Hill.

Una vista nocturna de Palm Desert desde Seven Level Hill.

Palm Desert: Vue de nuit depuis Seven Level Hill.

Nächtlicher Blick auf Palm Desert vom Seven Level Hill aus.

28

Trio of native palms stand guard over a desert knoll, Indio Hills.

Tres palmas nativas, como centinelas, en una loma desértica.

Un trío de palmiers de Californie monte la garde sur un
monticule désertique, Indio Hills.

Drei Palmen halten Wache über eine kahle Kuppe im Indio-Gebirge.

29

Crown of dawn over Little San Bernardinos.

El amanecer sobre Little San Bernardinos.

L'aube couronne glorieusement les petites San Bernardinos.

Vollendeter Sonnenaufgang über den Little-San-Bernardinos-Bergen.

Colorful Sand Verbena greets fellow denizens in spring, Thousand Palms Oasis.

La colorida Sand Verbena saluda las demás plantas en la primavera, Thousand Palms Oasis.

Les couleurs vives de la Verveine des Sables acceuillent les autres plantes régionales
au printemps, Thousand Palms Oasis.

Bunte Sandverbena grüßen im Frühjahr ihre Nachbarpflanzen in der Oase Thousand Palms.

31

Joshua Tree *Yucca brevifolia* detail.

Detalle de un Joshua Tree, *Yucca brevifolia*.

Le Joshua Tree *Yucca brevifolia*. Gros plan.

Eine Yucca brevifolia aus der Nähe.

Abundant irrigation sustains lush green crops in cultivation near Coachella.

Irrigación abundante mantiene verdes a los cultivos cerca de Coachella.

Grâce à une irrigation abondante, les cultures de Coachella
restent verdoyantes et luxuriantes.

Reichliche Bewässerung sichert die frisch-grüne Ernte
beim Gemüseanbau von Coachella.

Dainty desert sunflower and Sand Verbena in colorful garland.

Delicados girasoles desérticos entretejidos con Sand Verbena
en una guirnalda colorida.

Délicat 'Soleil' du désert et Verveine des Sables en
guirlandes de couleurs.

Zierliche Wüstensonnenblumen und Sandverbena bilden
eine bunte Girlande.

34

Mixed haze is funneled into the north valley
over San Gorgonio Pass.

Bruma mixta es encauzada hacia la parte norte del
valle a través de San Gorgonio Pass.

Les brumes mélées s'infiltrent dans la vallée du Nord
au-dessus du Col Gorgonio.

Ein Gemisch aus Dunst und Wolken verzieht sich in das nördliche Tal
über den San-Gorgonio-Paß.

A near constant breeze fuels windmill power plants
near North Palm Springs.

Una brisa casi constante activa los molinos y las centrales
eléctricas cerca de North Palm Springs

Une brise presque constante alimente les champs de
moulins à vent au nord de Palm Springs.

Die fast ständige Brise treibt das Windmühlenkraftwerk
nördlich von Palm Springs an.

Expansive views of the desert may be enjoyed while breathing frigid
pine-scented air from atop Mt. San Jacinto.

Vistas expansivas del desierto pueden apreciarse desde la cima de Mt. San Jacinto
mientras se respira el aire frio, con olor a pino.

Du sommet des montagnes San Jacinto, dans l'air glacé et embaumé
de la senteur des pins, on apprécie une très large vue du désert.

Ein weiter Blick auf die Wüset ist von der Spitze des San Jacinto aus xu genießen,
während man dort die kalte, nach Kiefern duftende Luft atmet.

38

Leafing Cottonwood heralds spring before snowy steeps, Chino Canyon.

Un alamo retoñando anuncia la llegada de primavera ante los nevados, Chino Canyon.

Le feuillage du peuplier Cottonwood annonce le printemps
devant les monts enneigés du Chino Canyon.

Die Cottonwood-Bäume setzen Blätter an, Anzeichen des Frühlings
vor schneebedeckten Hängen im Chino Canyon.

Icy water at rest in a distant world high above the desert
floor, San Jacinto Wilderness.

Aguas heladas y tranquilas en un mundo distante y muy
elevado del suelo desértico, San Jacinto Wilderness.

Calme des eaux gelées d'un monde lointain, très haut
au-dessus du niveau du désert. Etendues sauvages
de San Jacinto.

Stehendes Eiswasser in einer fernen Welt hoch über dem
Wüstengrund in der San-Jacintos-Wilderness.

One of a myriad of desert greens dedicated to the golfing enthusiast.

Una de muchas áreas verdes desérticas dedicadas a los
entusiastas del golf.

Une des multiples étendues de verdure du désert
consacrée aux fanatiques de golf.

Eine der unzähligen Grünflächen für den Golfspieler.

The Living Desert is 1200 acres of preserved desert exotica, including
Indian culture, wildlife and botanic gardens.

The Living Desert consiste de 1200 acres de exótica desértica
preservada que incluye fauna, jardines botánicos, y cultura india.

Le parc du Living Desert s'étend sur 485 hectares et offre tous les
éléments exotiques du désert. Culture indienne, faune et
flore sauvages et jardins botaniques y sont préservés.

Die Living Desert besteht aus 480 Hektar Land, wo das Ureigenste
der Wüste erhalten bleibt, einschließlich ihrer Indianerkultur,
ihres Tierlebens und botanischer Gärten.

42

Balloonists, sometimes in droves, delight in gliding over the peaceful desert landscape.

Aeronautas, a veces por docenas, se deleitan volando sobre el tranquilo paisaje desértico.

Glisser en ballon au-dessus des paysages tranquilles du désert est un plaisir que
l'on peut aussi apprecier en groupe.

Ballonsportler, manchmal in großer Zahl, erfreuen sich am Schweben
über der friedlichen Wüstenlandschaft.

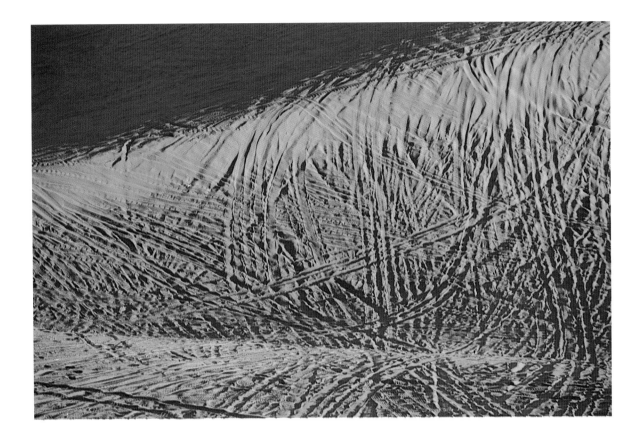

43

Evening respite for sands scarred by off-road enthusiasts.

Descanso vespertino para las arenas cicatrizadas por
entusiastas de vehículos recreacionales.

La fin de journée marque un répit pour les sables
sillonnés par les amateurs de tout-terrain.

Abendruhe über den Sandfurchen, die abwegige
Touristen hinterlassen haben.

44 - 45

Wonderland of Rocks area, Joshua Tree National Monument.

Wonderland of Rocks, Joshua Tree National Monument

Splendeurs des paysages de rochers. Joshua Tree National Monument.

Das Gebiet der ,,Wonderland of Rocks'' im Josua-Tree-National-Monument-Park.

46

Beavertail and Palo Verde in the Chocolate Mountains, sunrise.

"Beavertail" y Palo Verde en Chocolate Mountains durante el amanecer.

Beavertail et Palo Verde dans les montagnes Chocolat. Lever de soleil.

Beavertail-Gebeisch und Palo-Verde-Baum in dir
Chocolate-Bergen bei Sonnenaufgang.

47

Surface waters of the Salton Sea are 225 feet below sea level.

Las aguas superficiales del Salton Sea están aproximadamente
a 225 pies bajo el nivel del mar.

La surface des eaux de la mer Salton est située à environ
68 mètres au-dessous du niveau de la mer.

Die Wasseroberfläche der Salton Sea liegt etwa
80 Meter unter dem Meeresspiegel.

48

Evaporating rains leave behind a mud mosaic, Mecca Hills.

Lluvias al evaporar dejan atrás un mosaico de lodo, Mecca Hills.

Les pluies laissent, en s'évaporant, une mosaique de boue. Mecca Hills.

Verdunstender Regen hinterläßt ein Mosaik aus
Schlamm an den Berghängen um Mecca.

49

Emerging blossom braves treacherous spines of *Ferocactus*.

Una flor desafía las peligrosas espinas del Ferocactus.

Pour fleurir, les boutons doivent braver les traitres épines du *Ferocactus*.

Aufgehende Blüte trotzt den trügerischen Stachein des Fero-Kaktus.

Yucca whipplei

Opuntia sp.

51

Young California Fan Palms join a previous generation in perpetuating
the life of California's only native palms, *Washingtonia filifera*.

Palmas nuevas se unen con previas generaciones de California Fan Palms
para perpetuar la única palma nativa de California:
Washingtonia filifera.

Les jeunes palmiers-éventails se joignent aux générations précédentes
et perpétuent la seule sorte de palmiers d'origine
californienne: le *Washingtonia filifera*.

Junge Fächerpalmen sorgen zusammen mit den älteren für den Fortbestand
der einzigen in Kalifornien einheimischen Palmenart,
der *Washingtonia filifera*.

52 / 53

Sand Verbena enlivens Indio Hills.

Sand Verbena aviva las colinas de Indio Hills.

La Verveine des Sables donne vie aux collines Indio.

Sandverbena-Blüten bringen Leben in die Hänge der Indio-Berge.

54

Yucca at Bighorn Overlook, Pines to Palms Highway.

Yucca en Bighorn Overlook, Pines to Palms Highway.

Yucca. Bighorn Overlook, autoroute de Pines to Palm.

Yucca am Bighorn Overlook, am Pines to Palms Highway.

55

Evenings flush over Pinto Mountains, Joshua Tree National Monument.

Resplandecientes colores sobre Pinto Mountains,
Joshua Tree National Monument.

Les montagnes Pinto s'empourprent des lumières du soir.
Joshua Tree National Monument.

Abendrot über dem Pinto-Gebirge, Joshua Tree National Monument.

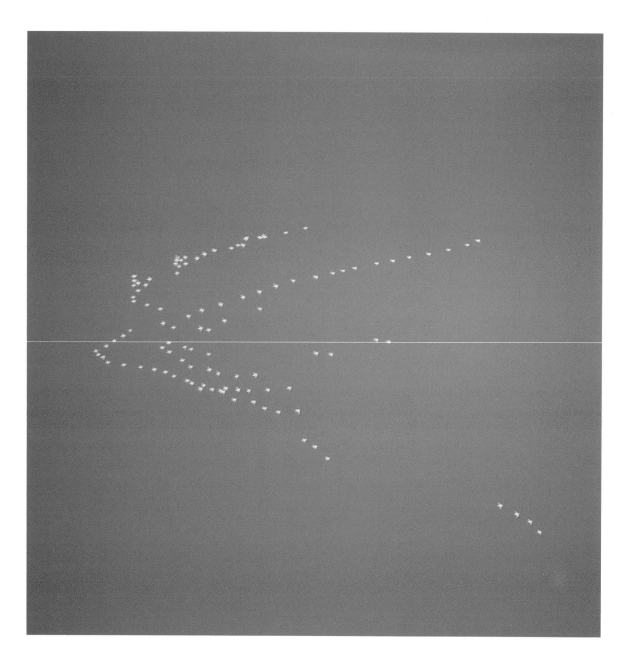

Gulls soar high above the Coachella Valley floor.

Gaviotas volando alto sobre Coachella Valley.

Mouettes haut dans le ciel de la vallée Coachella.

Möwen schweben hoch über dem Talgrund von Coachella.

57

Lopsided Yellow Pine oversees evergreen family in
Mt. San Jacinto State Park.

Un pino amarillo torcido vigila a una familia de pinos en
Mt. San Jacinto State Park.

Tout penchés, les pins jaunes surveillent les autres arbres à
feuilles persistantes dans le Parc d'Etat du San Jacinto.

Schiefe Gelbkiefer überragt eine Nadelholzgruppe
im Mount-San-Jacintos-Park.

58

Precious liquid greens the trees and banks lining Chino Canyon Creek.

Precioso líquido enverdece a los árboles y a la
orilla de Chino Canyon Creek.

De précieux liquides permettent la verdeur des arbres qui
cernent Chino Canyon Creek.

Kostbares Naß läßt Bäume und Ufer längs des Chino Canyon Creek ergrünen.

59

Mesquite provides summer verdance in the Grotto area, Orocopia Mountains.

El Mesquite mantiene su verdor durante el verano en el Grotto, Orocopia Mountains.

L'arbre Mesquite est une source de verdure durant l'été dans la région
des Grottes. Montagnes Orocopia.

Mesquite-Bäume kleiden die sogenannte Grotte im
Orocopia-Gebirge in sommerliches Grün.

60

Shrub and taproot bared by flow of Box Canyon wash
with Smoke Tree frame.

Un matorral con raíz descubierta por la corriente aluvial de
Boxcanyon; un Smoke Tree en el fondo.

Buissons et racines sont dénudés par les eaux
dans les fonds du Box Canyon.

Ein Rauchbaum umrahmt Büsche und Pfahlwurzeln, die das
Schwemmwasser aus dem Box Canyon bloßgelegt hat.

61

Bared Palo Verde branches in Box Canyon.

Ramas escuetas de Palo Verde en Box Canyon.

Branche dénudée de Palo Verde dans le Box Canyon.

Kahle Palo-Verde-Zweige im Box-Canyon.

62

Floral bouquet in low desert wash, Mecca Hills.

Ramillete de flores en el desierto bajo, Mecca Hills.

Arrangement floral dans les basses terres du désert. Mecca Hills.

Blumenbouquet im niederen Wüstenschwemmland, Mecca Hills.

63

Yellow blossoms on Palo Verde and vineyard below the Santa Rosa Mountains.

Flores amarillas de Palo Verde y una viña junto a las montañas Santa Rosa.

Fleurs d'or des jaunets sur fond de Palo Verde et de vignobles.
Pied des montagnes Santa Rosa.

Gelbblühende Palo-Verde-Bäume und Weinberge unterhalb des Santa-Rosa-Gebirges.

Pure white Desert Primrose enhances alluvial slope.

Primaveras desérticas blancas adornan una cuesta aluvial.

La pureté de la blanche primevère du désert embellit les pentes alluviales.

Schneeweiße Wüstenschlüsselblume an angeschwemmtem Abhang.

65

Glistening Salton Sea and eventide view of the
Santa Rosa Mountains.

La resplandeciente Salton Sea y las siluetas
de las montañas Santa Rosa al anochecer.

Eclats de la 'mer' de Salton au calme plat.
En fond, les montagnes Santa Rosa.

Abendlicher Blick auf die schimmernde Salton Sea
und das Santa-Rosa-Gebirge.

Ferocactus

67

Water and palms in Andreas Canyon provide the
elements of a desert oasis.

El agua y las palmas en Andreas Canyon proveen los
elementos necesarios de un oasis desértico.

Grâce à l'écoulement de l'eau qui abreuve les palmiers du
canyon Andrea, tous les éléments typiques d'un
véritable oasis sont ici réunis.

Im Andreas-Canyon nährt das fließende Wasser die einheimischen
Palmen und vollendet das Bild einer echten Oase.

Young green dates will require long weeks of intense
summer heat to bring them to maturity.

Estos tiernos dátiles verdes requerirán largas
semanas de calor veraniego para madurar.

_es jeunes dates vertes ne parviendront à maturité qu'après
de longues semaines d'intense chaleur estivale.

Junge grüne Datteln erfordern bis zur vollen Reife
wochenlange intensive Sommerhitze.